To Dana who was the love of my life and I will carry him with me always. But, as I move on and continue life's journey without my partner, I know you have your hands on me every step of the way. Rest in Paradise until we me again.

To God who blessed me with a loving mother and my children.

To my mother Rose Johnston and my God-fearing stepfather Milton Price.

To the blessing of those people that have been there with me always: Vanessa Anderson, Pricilla Ashmore, Tina Bastardo, Delores Mays, Ricky Kelly, Michelle Rucker, Glen Powell and a very special thanks to my dear sweet friend Donna Sbrogna Bernard who has made my dreams come true with her kindness.

Savior

One who has given life for me.
For in the end, my soul will be set free.
Savior saved me from all
My sin; when you have him, you will always win.

(Eternity)

Eyes

Your eyes have been open today.
All God's beauty is here to stay.
He has opened your eyes so
That you may see all that is given for you to achieve.

(The Gift)

I Am Not Ashamed

The world was given his son.
He gave him for us this race to run.
For on the cross for all to see
Jesus bled his life for you and me.
Some are ashamed and will not call your name.
I am so glad you love me, and this is my gain.

(The Cross)

Alive

I am alive because you died for me.
I am alive because you loved me.
I am alive because you took the cross to Calvary.
I am alive because you live in me.

(My Lord)

Time

Time does not stand still.
Time is God's will.
Time does not sit on a shelf.
Time is all by itself.
We tend to ask God for more time.
He had asked us in the beginning to let him in; we denied him.
Now that our end is near,
We want God to hear,
For death is knocking.
This is clear.
Time has run out.

(The End)

Caring

Love that is shown.
Loving his word, we must make it known.
Love coming from one's heart, that is the way caring starts.

(Love)

Today

You were awakened by the sun.
A new day has begun.
Father has blessed you, answered your prayers
With a night angel he had sent as you slept
While other eyes he had met.
For he saw the pain that we did not see; those eyes
That did not see, those eyes that did not open now sit with thee.
Foolish things should not matter,
For life is short for all that chatter.
Let's be thankful for today.
For God's love is always.

           (The Promise)

Prayers

The key to one's soul.
Prayers always heard by God.
Prayers so dear and sweet
Prayers God's ears always meet.

        (Answers)

Father

Father from above.
Father, I'm glad it's me you love.
Father, from my mouth to your ears
I will make it very clear.
My love for you is true, and my heart I give to you.
Father, I ran such a race.
Still you stopped me and gave me your grace.

        (A Parent)

Repentance

Asking God to come in your heart.
Repentance is when you do not walk alone.
Repentance is when you want to make change.
Repentance has no dry eyes.
Repentance is when you cry.

(The Heart)

Daily Assignment

Prayer is the opening of the day.
Thanking God for your stay.
Being thankful for your morning joy and all its blessing,
Did not have to ask God for his second-guessing.

(Homework)

Pain

Jesus took it all and stood great, mighty, and tall.
Nailed to the cross with pain,
He gave his life for our gain.
We must never forget that day,
For he gave his life for our stay.

(Favored)

Being a Christian

It's hard.
We make mistakes.
We mess up.
We sin.
What is great in being a Christian is that
We have Jesus and we will always win.

        (Amen)

Gemstone

Beautiful, they are.
They need to be polished from time to time.
While polishing, there may be some friction,
Because we are not perfected without adversity.
Let's continue to be like that gemstone
And to continue to shine and not rest his desire to make change.

(Beauty)

Traveling

Life is nothing but a traveling station.
We make many stops along life's way.
From place to place, sea to sea,
Traveling through life is a breeze.

       (Wind)

Mothers

So beautiful and vibrant.
In early years, taking care of her family is truly clear.
Stories she will tell about how her life began.
As she speaks, she never dwells.
As I look upon the frail gray-haired woman as she.
Still remember Mother and still as vibrant to me.

(My Blessing)

Tomorrow

They are never promised; we must be thankful,
For our todays for tomorrow may never come.

(Live)

Beauty

Skies are blue
Grass is green
Earthy smells
Ever so clean
Eyes shut
For they see
All beauty in their dreams.

(Blind)

Mercies

There at the cross
For there, Jesus's life was lost.
Mercies thankful
We shall be; God gave his only son to bleed.
Shed his blood at the cross,
His life was our final cost.

                (Alpha)

Destination

Destined to live in this world, you see, Noah
God gave to help us to be relieved.
Forty days
Forty night
God kept Noah in his sight.
A dove went out to find land.
Noah rested in Jesus's hands.

(Found)

Children

Life's blessings from above
God gave us children to care and love.

      (Creation)

A Storm Is Coming

A storm is coming; are you ready?
A storm is coming; are you listening to God's words?
A storm is coming; are you reaching out to others
Before the storm comes?
A storm is coming; there will be nowhere to run.
Keep on building and let all know,
For the rain will come and all will be washed away.
Heaven will shine, and it will be a brand-new day.

(Afterglow)

Whispers

Words so sweet,
Words are the hearts that are deep.
Hearts will be as one, will soon know life has begun.
Uniting love so true that God has made for two.
Soon there will be patters of little feet
By hearing God's whispers ever so sweet.

      (Unity)

Strength

When you're weary,
Feeling blue,
Call on Jesus.
He will get you through.
Ask for his strength to help within.
Calling on Jesus,
You will always win.

(Help)

Listen

Hear ye, hear ye;
I come to bring good news.
Open your hearts and see me through.
My words are true, for I fell in love with you.
Come with me, and we shall live eternally.

(Forever)

Streets of Gold

Walking with our feet on golden streets,
No more crying, no more pain, souls are free because you came.
As you walk alongside me, telling me what we all wanted to hear,
We kept our mouth silent, so you made it very clear.
The streets are golden,
For we all believed you were true.
Now we walk the streets of gold with you.

(Believe)

Raised

From the tomb you were raised,
Mark of the thorns in your head.
Put into the tomb, you were dead.
Three days you appeared with scars for all to see.
We will live 'cause Jesus is the victory.

        (Saved)

Night Falls

Hustle and bustle of the day,
Night has fallen this way.
Time to put the day away and rest.
God will plant dreams for your mind to wonder.
He will keep watch as you sleep, counting
Sheep, and will wake you with his sunlight with
    the morning greet.

(Faithful)

Life's Journey

Place to place,
Shore to shore,
Different times,
Land to sea,
Life is life
For you and me.

Morning Joy

I wake in the morning
After a nightlong slumber.
God has given me a day to wonder.
When I look to the skies and see heaven's eyes,
I know my Lord has filled me with morning joy.

(The Blessing)

Life

The precious gift from God.
Embrace the life that God so freely gives.
Give thanks as you live and breathe,
For God's love is never deceived.

    (God's Love)

God's Love to You

He sent his only son to die on the cross

He has shown us how to rise above
Because he has given us such love.
What an awesome God we serve.

       (Thank you, Lord!)

Peace

Peace is the calm that comes from within.
Peace is to release the world's daily winds
To find one's calm that is in your heart.
Jesus said, "Follow me. From you I will never part."

(Our Savior)

Feelings

If you can feel, hear, touch, then you know God exists.
Seek him, find him,
For he is our earthly glow.
His love is real,
For his Bible tells us so.

(Grace)

God Said No Stress

Walk with me and I will give you the rest.
Ask of me and I will release your stress.
Lay your burdens down for I will bless.
I will give you nothing but the best.
As you stay on bending knees,
I will hear your request.

(Jesus)

Shining Light

Lord, keep shining
Your light ever so bright.
Shine with the glow for others to see,
Because that shining light
May just be the light someone needs.

(God's Light)

Problems

Problems—some big, some small,
God does handle all through his loving arms.
He will proclaim you can feel his presence.
He is always there because he cares.
All your problems he will bear to let you know he is there.

(Caring)

Breathe

Relax, take the day as it comes to a stop.
Focus, take time to breathe.
God has you no matter what.
So relax and breathe; God has your breath.

       (Release)

Hearing God

Life you have given unto me.
My hands shall prosper.
My eyes shall observe.
My ears shall hear your every word.
My lips shall speak of your love.
My heart will beat because it all comes from above.

(Savior)

Sorrows

Sorrows come with life and death.
Sorrows will bring on tomorrows.
Sorrows will bring on life's salvation.
Through thick and thin,
When we know Jesus, we will always win.

(Hope)

Lost Souls

People who walk in darkness
They have no shadow

       (Seeking Light)

My First Love

You have given me your only son.
You brought joy to my life.
By giving a life, you have taken me
From a world of darkness
And brought light into my soul.
You said, "Trust in me. I will give the rest."
For this I know, for I am blessed.
You have my heart, for I will not depart.
I trust in you, for you are my first love.

(Jesus)

Troubled Waters

Stormy waters will come
From time to time.
A downpour of rain will come.
You will have some highs,
Some lows—God already knows.
For your struggles are life's true lessons and God's blessings.
Staying faithful and true,
God will calm your waters, for this is true.

        (Patient)

Worth

People have saying being about something.
A child of God is more than something.
You are loved from the most high, looking above in heaven's eyes.
Yes, yes, kings and queens about something of the most high.
Walk with pride for about something Jesus is inside.

(Arrived)

Tolerance

Lord, give us the strength for the day's life test,
For I will put my trust in you, for I am blest
As the days go on.
I am thankful for your grace and mercies,
For you have met all of my needs.

(Deliver)

Choosing the Right Words

Think before you speak.
Words can be very harmful.
Choose words correctly before leaving one's lips,
For loose lips sink ships, and ships will not be back
Afloat once that boat has sunk.

(Wisdom)

Missing Loved Ones

We mourn, we cry when loved ones have gone.
God has seen their pain beyond.
He saw that they were done with earthly repair,
So he lifted them up, and they are in his care.
We had to let them go, for Jesus said so.
They are on the other side as Jesus promised this is why he died.
They will wait by and by.

(Gone Home)

Loving Oneself

God said, "Love oneself."
God said, "Be true to oneself."
God said, "Encourage oneself."
God said, "To strive is to love oneself."
God said, "Walk proud, oneself."
For nobody knows oneself like thyself.

(Truth)

Being Thankful

Make every waking day count.
Know the love and joy that God has given.
Know whatever your day brings, God is in full control of all
    your destiny.
Praise his name, Jesus.
Thank him for this day, for you are truly blessed.

(Grateful)

Embrace

Embrace your life.
Embrace your loved ones.
Embrace your gifts.
Embrace the day that you are given.
Embrace all from above.
Embrace God's eternal love.

                (Gifts)

Rainbow

A rainbow is God's window to one's soul.
After a morning shower of rain,
You can see the rainbow of glow of yellow,
The warmth of the sun
Blue, the beauty of sky,
For all to see green God's earth for all plant and life to grow
That warms the hearts after a morning dew
With the sun shining forever through.

        (Life)

Praising His Name

Jesus died for you and me.
Jesus carried his cross for all to see.
Jesus—his blood he shed.
Jesus is left for dead.
Jesus is placed in a tomb.
Jesus's hands have open wounds.
Jesus, I am praising your name.
Jesus, I am so glad you came.

(The Messiah)

Getting Ready

Are you ready?
These are the last days.
We shall see our Maker in all his glory.
He paid the price so all shall live eternal life.
God is knocking for your life to be saved.
He wants to save you from that eternal grave.

(Blessings)

Paradise

Passengers here on earth, we are.
We are going through until the train's last, final call.
God gave us his words to read, and at the end of revelations, he will retrieve.
He is the beginning, the end.
This we know, for we are heaven-bound, our last show.
There is light there for all that shine,
For his will was done and all glory divine.
As we keep our faith,
God shall see our eternal rest is with him.
God took us through earthly test if we kept his commandments.
We are at rest for we are heaven-bound.

(Alpha and Omega)

Flowers

Red, yellow, green, blue
God's springtime colors coming through
Sending sweet smell ever so sweet
Around summers, come to meet.

(Beauty)

Clouds

Among the blue skies
White and puffy as the earth moves slowly by
When two connect, rain shall fall, but the
    clouds stay puffy through it all.

(Movement)

Stars

Shining ever so bright,
Stars, you will be my light tonight,
As I look up and see you sparkle with gleam,
As I sit in a midnight's dream.

               (Light)

Seeds

Water me, I will grow.
Reading God's word tells you so,
For in his garden, he planted seeds.
He wants them watered by you and me.

        (Growth)

Near

Jesus is near.
Have no fear.
He made it very clear.
Time has come for this world to be done.
If you need a ride, Jesus is knocking; let him inside.
Jesus is near.

(The Coming)

My Everything

I have loved you from the start.
My love for you will not depart.
I pray every day of my life you will stay.
On the cross you said it was finished—that's when life began,
    that day.

                    (All)

Heaven

Where the angels sing,
Heaven is where bells ring.
Heaven is where life begins.
Heaven has no end.
Heaven we shall see.
Heaven is for all who believe.

(Home)

Flight

Soaring through worldly life.
Flying every day's flight.
Final days are getting near.
Hope all know Jesus when he appears.

        (Leaving)

Intimacy

Intimacy in my womb.
Intimacy made for two.
Intimacy was God's plan.
Intimacy for woman and man.
Intimacy—now that I have you in my hand—
    was knitted by God,
The master—and oh, how grand.

    (The Master)

Baby

Precious joy
Baby girl or boy
Baby so beautiful to see.
Baby was once you and me.

(The Nature)

Blowing in the wind

You can feel me, but you cannot see me.
I make you shiver when my strength is at full force.
I will get to many lengths as dust will twirl and you will swirl.
Hats will fly as my winds go high.
Still you cannot see me.
I am just blowing in the wind.

       (Feel)

Life's Partner

Husband, husband, where can you be?
God brought you home, away from me.
He saw you were sick, and no more your body could take,
So he brought you home for heaven's sake.
We will meet in another time.
I do thank God for a love divine.
For you, my love, will always be.
Heaven is your home, and you are free.

(My Heart)

Across

Through the sand and through seas,
Jesus walks on water for you and me.

>   (Weathering Storms)

Son

You roam the streets alone.
Nowhere to turn to but to go home.
You felt unwanted.
You're so far from truth.
For mother has loved you from your youth.
You took the streets home.
You could not bear; all you found was danger there.
Mother is crying.
You are not alone; her arms are waiting for you to come home.

(A Mother's Love)

Emptiness

Like a glass sitting on a shelf,
With life wonders all by itself.
Day and night goes by.
You sit and sigh, why is my glass empty?
Alone, sitting on the shelf all by itself.
Jesus said, "Call on me.
I will fill your glass and set you free."
My glass is full now, you see.
For Jesus came that day and sat with me.

(Full)

When

Shall the loneliness end?
When will my heart sing again?

    (Searching the Heart)

Alive

I am alive because you died for me.
I am alive because you love me.
I am alive because you took the cross to Calvary.
I am alive for you live in me.

       (Living)

Dying

Standing once tall
Till sickness came and took it all.
Your time has come
For your deep sleep,
For your earthly life has been complete.
As you lie and wait,
Jesus will be picking up his date to be his bride side-by-side,
Going to heaven for the final ride.

(The Wedding)

A Song

There's a song in my heart
That Jesus and I will never part.
Praising his name, glory to thee
Jesus, my King, this is why I sing.

                    (Joy)

Caring

Love comes from within.
That is where it all begins.
We must make it known
To have God's love shown.
It all comes from the heart.
That is where caring starts.

(Unity)

Windows

They are the glass to one's soul.
Sometimes they get broken, everyone knows.
As we are bending to fill and mend,
We must not go on pretending
That souls sometimes are lost in deep holes.

(Finding a Way Out)

Getting Old

Once young, full of fun,
Slowly graying, drifting and swaying.
Getting closer to our Maker,
God gives a sign for the undertaken.
He lets us know if it's time to rest.
For soon you'll be in the arms of the best.

(Relationship)

Love

The feeling of one's heartbeat
When there are two, such love will do.
Hands holding ever so sweet
While together with one heartbeat.
As eyes lock with a love so true,
This is why I feel this love so real.

              (Sharing)

Hold On!

Stay strong.
Jesus took the cross so all would not be lost.
Stressful day, sleepless nights,
Jesus said, "Never give up the fight."

(Life)

Another Place and Time

Life would be different if you were mine,
If we would have met in another place and time.
Love cannot be,
For your heart belongs to another who loves thee.
I will always wonder from time to time
If we would have met in another place and time.

(Mystery)

I Do Love You

Prayed for your love and you sent it from above.
Lord, I will never let you go.
For your love for me I always need so.
I do love you, this is true.
I am so happy my heart has found you.

(Love)

The Womb

As I lay in my mother's womb,
So warm and growing, I will be born soon
To come into the world to see what life has in store for me.
Out of the womb I came looking around and seeing all the pain.
I said this world is not for me.
Full of hate and so much crime
I said, "Lord, this is not my time."
Full of gloom and all doom.
Lord, I want to be back safe in my mother's womb.

(Comfort)

Sisters

Your first best friend.
Sisters love you without end.
Sisters always by your side.
Sisters will be there when you cry.
Sisters getting old and gray.
Gabriel's horn blows; you must go away.
Sisters always in my heart.
Sisters, we will never part.
God, I want to thank you for my sisters that you lent me.
For they were a gift from heaven.

(Family)

Sodom and Gomorrah

God said, "Leave the swine; there is nothing there but crime."
Do not look back, he said, for stone will turn.
Sodom and Gomorrah were burned.
God is coming again because he said Sodom and Gomorrah are
    becoming a trend.
Ready or not, fire will come.
God is saying this world is done.

      (The End)

Giving

A child was born.
His mother knew his life would be torn
Into the world, teaching all that he knew.
Knowing his life will be gone in a few,
Carrying the cross he has to bear.
He knew that his father was there.
He said, "It is written, my son."
Now the world's life has begun.

              (The Son)

The Sun

Shining in the morning glow
The Son warm and comforting for all to know
The Son so glory divine
His love is with us all the time.
When night comes the Sun fades
For the Son has given another day

      (Light Ahead with the Son)

Sleeping

Closing my eyes, not knowing where I go,
You keep watch over my soul.
Relaxed is my body as I sleep.
I drift off ever so sweet.
I wonder, where do I go?
As I close my eyes and breathe slow,
I awake for another day.
You slept beside me all the way.

(Angel Kept Watch)

Father

In my life you came.
You showed me love, and what a gain.
You held my hand as I walked down the aisle to be wed.
You called me your child.
You told me you had to go.
I said I will be OK, this I so know; we said our last goodbyes
    with tears in your eyes.
You said, "Take care of your mother, for you will
    never get another.
My time is near.
I love you, dear.
Jesus awaits at the pearly gates."

    (My Dad Loves You)

About the Author

Diane Ashmore is a widow, a mother of three and two stepchildren, a grandmother of many grandchildren, and a great-grandmother to three great-grandchildren. She is truly blessed. She loves the Lord and thanks him for such a beautiful journey of life that he has given her so far. Although her husband was taken sooner than she wanted, God blessed Diane with this talent to write from her heart. She hopes that as a reader of her work that she is blessed with, it will help to inspire you. May God bless and keep you all. Amen.

CPSIA information can be obtained
at www.ICGtesting.com
Printed in the USA
FFOW03n1845240418
46331929-47914FF